Reading Beyond the Basal®

AROUND THE WORLD

POLAND

THE WOODEN DOLL
SUSAN BONNERS

Teacher Guide by Barbara Valdez

*Using Children's Literature
to Learn About Cultures*

Perfection Learning

Editor-in-Chief: Kathleen Myers
Senior Editor: Mary Jo Cosson
Editor: Susan C. Thies
Designers: Tamera Diggs-Tate
Deborah Lea Bell
Inside Illustration: Donald E. Tate II

Consultant

Professor Jadwiga Kołodziejska
Warsaw, Poland

About the Author

Barbara Valdez works with primary-level children as a reading consul-
tant in the Washington Unified School District, West Sacramento,
California. At American River College, Sacramento, she is the instructor
in reading methods for student tutors who work each day with elementary school children. Ms. Valdez is also on the faculty of St. Mary's
College, Moraga, California. A former elementary teacher, reading spe-
cialist, principal, and district curriculum director, Ms. Valdez is an
active member of her local reading council and past president of the
California Reading Association. She is also a former member of the
Board of Directors of the International Reading Association.

NOTE: Due to the rapidly changing social situation in eastern Europe,
the author and publisher apologize for the possibility of outdated
information.

Dear Friends,

In these times when the rapidity of air travel and television are bringing us closer together on the great blue globe, literature presents an opportunity to share cultures visually and interactively with other people. The study of cultures, including their history and geography, is important to us as teachers and models for our children. There is no better way to look at other cultures from a distance than through their literature.

Language, songs and dances, and family and ethnic rituals are all a part of learned behavior that makes up a culture. Children from one culture should be learning about other cultures in order to avoid ethnocentrism and to help open the doors to communication. When children live in a world with mutual understanding and acceptance of differences among world neighbors, we will have a world of peace.

The literature selections in this series present opportunities to learn about other people and places. The children will be enriched by learning about other children. Those of us who are teachers will aid in carrying the good words of love, peace, and communication among neighbors and friends.

The stories are enjoyable and will help us more clearly understand cultural values. This understanding will help us take an active role in building positive and loving bridges between cultures. Children learn by example, so put your heart into reading the book and completing selected activities, and we will help our children become better world neighbors.

There can be peace and understanding among children, and it will begin with us.

Barbara Valdez

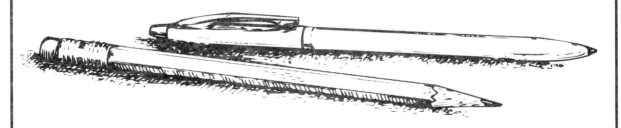

Contents

About...

This Guide 6
The Story 7
The Author and Illustrator. 9
The Dedication 10

Reader/Book Links

Introducing the Book 11
Getting to Know the Characters. 12
Discussing the Setting/Time 13
Exploring the Theme 14

Language Considerations

Literary Devices 15
Picture Analysis 15
Oral Language 16
Writing 17

Geography of Poland

A World View 18
A Closer Look 18
    Poland, the Country 19
    Warsaw, the Capital City 23

Polish Cultural Connections

Polish Language 24
Polish Music 27
Polish Art 29
Polish Education 32
Polish Food/Cooking 34
Polish Holidays/Celebrations 37
Polish Recreation. 40

Polish Cultural Extensions 44

Annotated Bibliography

Books 46
Folktales 49
Teacher References 51
Polish Recordings 51

Fact Sheet on POLAND Reproducible. 53
Fact Sheet on WARSAW Reproducible 57
Map of Poland Reproducible 58
Kinga's Dowry Reproducible 59
Polish Language Reproducible 60
The Sea Captain Reproducible 61
The Four Clever Sisters Reproducible 67
Polish Embroidery Motif Reproducible 70
Leluja Wycinanki Reproducible 71
Gwiazdy Wycinanki Reproducible 72
Potatoes with Cheese Jackets Recipe Reproducible . . 73
Red Cabbage and Apple Salad Recipe Reproducible. . 74
Barszcz Recipe Reproducible 75
Kapusniak Recipe Reproducible 76
Poppy Seed Cake Recipe Reproducible 78
Noodles with Poppy Seeds Recipe Reproducible 79
Pisanki Reproducible 80

About This Guide

Children's literature can transport students to distant countries with cultures and traditions far removed from their own. By reading books from faraway places, students become acquainted with cultural differences. At the same time, though, students also will begin to recognize the many similarities among cultures. This guide has been designed to accompany the featured book with the direct purpose of helping you introduce students to the culture represented within the story.

Begin this unique cultural study with the sharing of *The Wooden Doll*, a contemporary fiction picture book set in Poland. Then use the book-related activities offered in the guide to help students begin to develop an understanding and appreciation of the country of Poland and its people. In this way, *The Wooden Doll* will become the scaffold upon which your students will be able to build new understandings and knowledge.

Once the book has been explored, use the guide to help your students continue to make cultural connections. The culture-related background information, geographical facts, and wide variety of activities and discussion questions will help you direct students in their investigation of the Polish language, music, art, clothing, food, celebrations, and recreation. Suggested extension topics will enable you to encourage students to continue their study. Also included is an annotated bibliography providing books and recordings for related reading and further research.

Through the study of cultures, your students will experience the different approaches various peoples have developed to handle situations common to all humankind. As a result, they will learn to accept and respect diversity and grow in understanding of themselves and others.

About the Story

The storyteller, Stephanie, tells the reader about a visit to her grandparents' home many years before. As she lies in the living room trying to fall asleep the first night of her visit, her gaze settles on Grandpa's beautiful wooden doll. During previous visits, Stephanie has longed to play with the painted doll sitting on the shelf next to the clock. But Grandpa has never let her touch it. "When you're older," he has always said.

Stephanie is sure she must be old enough by now. So she follows Grandpa around outside the next morning until the time is right to ask him about his wooden doll. Grandpa tells her the doll is not for playing. When Stephanie insists, Grandpa becomes stern.

That afternoon while Grandma and Grandpa are napping, Stephanie's desire to hold the mysterious wooden doll over-powers her better judgment. Quietly, she climbs on a chair and takes the beautiful doll from the tall shelf. As Stephanie gingerly examines the painted doll, she is surprised to discover several smaller dolls nested inside. She counts ten different dolls in all!—the smallest no bigger than a peanut. Best of all, she finds *Stephania* written on the bottom of the biggest doll. She is sure Grandpa must be saving the doll for her.

Grandma discovers what Stephanie has done before she has a chance to return the doll to the shelf. Although she is disappointed that Stephanie has disobeyed, Grandma encourages her to ask Grandpa again about the doll. When he hears from Stephanie that she has seen her name on the bottom, Grandpa decides to share the doll's interesting story with her.

"You were named after my mother," Grandpa tells Stephanie. "That is her name on the bottom of the doll." Grandpa explains that the nesting dolls were a special gift to his mother from his father. Then he continues by

describing his early years in Poland and the small farm where he lived. He tells Stephanie that his mother gave him the dolls to bring with him to America when he left Poland as a young man. Grandpa's story is one that could be told by many immigrants to the New World. With the story, Grandpa also gives Stephanie the doll. "We'll keep her here for you when you visit," Grandpa tells her.

About the Author and Illustrator

Susan Bonners was born in Chicago, Illinois. She received her early art training from her mother, who worked as a commercial artist for Montgomery Ward. After earning her B.A. in English from Fordham University, she attended art school in New York City.

Ms. Bonners has written and illustrated a number of children's books. She is very innovative with the variety of mediums she uses in her illustrations. *Panda* was the first book she wrote as well as illustrated. It describes the habits of the panda in poetic, hand-lettered text. *Panda* is illustrated in shades of blue watercolor with blurred edges to create soft pictures. Her book *A Penguin Year* received the American Book Award in 1982. Other books she has illustrated include *Sarah's Questions* by Harriet Ziefert and her own wordless picture book, *Just in Passing*. *The Wooden Doll* was inspired by Ms. Bonners' own childhood and her fascination with a wooden nesting doll that her grandfather had brought with him from Poland.

Ms. Bonners currently lives in Brooklyn, New York.

About the Dedication

The dedication for *The Wooden Doll* reads: "To my grandparents—and to all those who left one world behind to make their way in another." Ask students what they think this dedication means. Discuss whether they think this is an appropriate dedication for this book and their reasons for feeling as they do.

READER/BOOK LINKS

Literature provides both a mirror in which students can see themselves and a window through which they can view the lives of others. When the literature represents another part of our world, readers have the additional opportunity to explore a new culture through the pages of a book. The following activities and questions are intended to help children connect with the book *The Wooden Doll*. Choose those that will be the most meaningful to your students.

Introducing the Book

Ask the students what they think about when the country of Poland is mentioned. List students' responses on the chalkboard or chart paper. Then ask students what they would like to learn about this country. List their questions and areas of interest. Save the recorded information so students can add to it as they gain knowledge. Refer to the list during the study of Poland and encourage students to observe how their ideas change and grow.

Provide students with a blank sheet of paper. Ask them to each draw a picture of what they imagine when they think about Poland. Students can draw a scene, person, map, or whatever they feel will represent Poland. Encourage the students to draw as much detail as possible. Save the drawings. Then at the end of the unit, ask students to repeat the assignment and compare their "before" and "after" drawings.

Show students the cover of the book and read the title and the author's name. Ask students what they think the little girl on the cover is holding. Explain that it is a nesting doll that the little girl's grandfather brought with him when he left his native country, Poland. Ask students if they or someone they know has traveled to Poland. Continue by asking students if they or someone they know has nesting dolls.

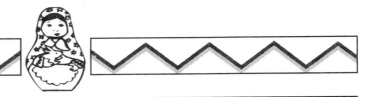

Point out the country of Poland on a world map or globe. Have students share what they can tell about Poland by looking at the map or globe.

- What continent is Poland in?

- Do you think the country of Poland is bigger or smaller than our country?

- What countries border Poland? What forms Poland's northern border?

Have students make some predictions about Poland and how the area compares with where they live.

Ask students if their grandparents, parents, or other family members have any items they keep on a shelf or in a special place. Discuss these items and why they are special.

Getting to Know the Characters

After sharing the book, choose from the following discussion questions.

- If the author is an adult now, when do you think this story takes place?

- Why do you think the wooden doll is so important to Grandpa?

- Do you think Grandma is from Poland? Why or why not?

- How old do you think Stephanie is in the story? How old do you think she is now? Explain your reasoning.

- Do you think Stephanie should have been punished for taking down the wooden doll when her grandfather told her not to?

- How are you like Stephanie and how are you

different? (Record or chart the similarities and differences students mention.)

- Are you enough like Stephanie that this book could have been written about you? Why or why not?

Discussing the Setting/Time

Remind students that Grandpa was born in Poland. Use a map and point out this country. Discuss with students where their ancestors are from. Encourage students to check at home for more information. Mount a large world map on the wall. Invite children to place tags with their names on appropriate countries to indicate the origins of their ancestors.

Ask students where and when they think this story takes place.

Discuss with students how old they think the wooden nesting dolls are.

Ask students if anything about the setting surprised them. If so, discuss why they were surprised. Invite students to describe something about where they live that might surprise Stephanie.

Discuss with students why they think Grandpa left Poland when he was seventeen years old.

Discuss with students whether they visit their grandparents. Ask students if there are special things kept just for them at their grandparents' house.

Exploring the Theme

In a picture book, the illustrations and text are very closely related. Ask students to study the illustrations carefully. Then have them explain how the theme of the book is depicted in the illustrations.

Ask students why they think Susan Bonners wrote this book.

Invite students to describe the theme in their own words. One possible theme might be that people's backgrounds or histories cause them to react differently to the various circumstances in their lives.

Remind students that Stephanie thought Grandpa was quiet because he had lived a very quiet and lonely childhood. Ask students whether they agree with Stephanie's thoughts about Grandpa. Then ask them to explain why they feel as they do.

Family values play an important part in this story. Even though Grandpa doesn't talk much to Stephanie and Grandma, ask students how they can tell that Grandpa values his life on the farm. How about Grandma? Ask students what they think she values and how they can tell.

LANGUAGE CONSIDERATIONS

Multicultural children's literature can be a powerful device to help students understand a world far from their own reality. The language of the book will help students learn more about Grandpa and his culture. This understanding will enable the students to begin making their own personal cultural connections.

Literary Devices

Remind students that the storyteller is the main character in the book. She is telling a story about herself. Explain that this writing technique is called *viewpoint* and that the author has written the book in *first person*. Display and read a sentence or two from a book written in third person. Discuss with students the advantages and the disadvantages of these two writing perspectives. Ask students why they think the author chose to write in first person for this book. Invite students to explain which writing perspective they prefer for their own writing and why. Encourage students to select a page from *The Wooden Doll* and rewrite it using third person.

Discuss with students how this story would be different if Grandma or Grandpa were writing it. Invite students to choose one of these two characters and rewrite an episode or a scene from that viewpoint.

Point out that Susan Bonners uses a lot of dialogue in *The Wooden Doll*. Ask students whether they think the use of dialogue makes a story more or less interesting. Encourage students to select a paragraph or two that contains a lot of dialogue and rewrite it using no dialogue.

Picture Analysis

Ask students to describe the artist's style—painting techniques, picture shapes and sizes, use of color, and so on. Discuss whether students think Ms. Bonners' style fits this

book. Have them explain their reasoning. Students might enjoy using poster paints to create a picture of the inside of a room in their house. Encourage them to use a lot of detail and make their paintings realistic, similar to Susan Bonners' style.

Suggest that students take a closer look at the pictures of Grandma and Grandpa's farm—inside and out. Have them list everything they can learn about the farm by studying the pictures.

Point out that *The Wooden Doll* is illustrated by the author. While most students are used to illustrating the books they write, encourage them to think about the advantages and disadvantages of illustrating their own work. Invite students to try using classmates to illustrate books they write.

Encourage students to study the picture of Grandma and Grandpa's kitchen on the title page. Discuss how it is similar to and different from the students' kitchens.

Have students look at the picture showing the basement of Grandma and Grandpa's house. List the items students can identify from the picture. Ask them to study how Grandma does the wash and compare it to how their families wash clothes.

Grandma tells Stephanie that Grandpa gets up early and works hard. Ask students to study the pictures and explain what they think Grandpa works hard at all day.

Students might enjoy creating their own sets of nesting dolls. Various-sized plastic containers—yogurt, cottage cheese, ice cream, and so on—could be used.

Oral Language

Suggest that students form groups of four and read *The Wooden Doll* aloud. Groups will need to decide who wants to be Grandpa, Grandma, Stephanie, and the narrator. Or invite students to create a Readers' Theater script for an episode of the book such as the first morning scene between Stephanie and Grandma, the garden scene between Stephanie and Grandpa, or the after-dinner scene with Grandma, Grandpa, and Stephanie.

Remind students that Grandpa tells Stephanie a little about his childhood in Poland. Invite students to work with a partner to develop questions they would like to ask Grandpa about his family and their life in Poland. Then encourage pairs to assume the roles of Grandpa and the interviewer, asking and answering the questions they have developed.

Arrange the class into small groups. Encourage them to discuss how they would feel about living on a farm in Poland such as Grandpa describes.

Writing

Suggest students write a letter from Stephanie to Grandpa and Grandma or from either Grandpa or Grandma to Stephanie once she returns home after her visit.

Grandpa left his family and his native country, Poland, when he was seventeen years old. Students might enjoy writing a story about Grandpa's life after he left Poland. Encourage students to carry their writing through all the steps of the writing process—prewriting, drafting, sharing, revising, editing, and publishing.

Have students write a poem about the painted wooden dolls.

Invite students to write a character description of Grandpa, Grandma, or Stephanie. Have them describe the character they choose to someone who hasn't read this book or seen any of the illustrations. Ask students to try to use some of the words from the story.

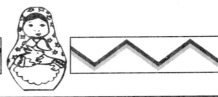

GEOGRAPHY OF POLAND

Choose from the following activities to help students gain a better understanding of the geographical features of the country of Poland.

A World View

Introduce students to this region by starting with the big picture. Students can gain a clearer image of Poland by seeing how it compares with the rest of the world.

Use a classroom map, an atlas, or a globe to point out the country of Poland. Compare Poland's location to where the students live. Explain that Poland is located on the continent of Europe. List the seven continents on the chalkboard: Africa, Antarctica, Asia, Australia, Europe, North America, and South America. Discuss how Europe compares in size to the other six continents.

Ask if any of the students or anyone they know has ever traveled to Poland. Talk about what route students would take to travel to Poland, what oceans or large bodies of water they would cross, how they would travel, and how long they think it would take to get there.

State the phrase "The world is getting smaller." Ask students what they think the phrase means. Once the meaning of the phrase has been established, ask students what personal implications this could have for them.

A Closer Look

Continue your study of this region by first taking a closer look at the country of Poland. A Fact Sheet on POLAND has been provided on pages 53-56. Then introduce your students to the city of Warsaw. A Fact Sheet on WARSAW has been included on page 57. You may wish to reproduce the fact sheets for discussion with the students or use the

information as teacher background. The following activities and discussion questions are provided to help students learn more about this interesting region.

Poland, the Country

Use the map of Poland provided on page 58 and make a large outline wall map or individual outline maps for the students. Encourage students to locate and label the following.

- **the surrounding countries of Byelorussian, Czechoslovakia, Germany, Lithuania, Slovakia, and Ukraine**

- **the Baltic Sea**

- **the cities of Bydgoszcz, Gdańsk, Katowice, Kraków, Lódź, Poznań, Szczecin, Warsaw, and Wrocław**

- **the Bug River and the Vistula River**

- **the Gulf of Danzig**

Use the map of Poland provided on page 58 and invite students to make individual maps showing the seven regions: the Baltic Lakes Region, the Carpathian Forelands, the Central Plains, the Coastal Lowlands, the Polish Uplands, the Sudetes Mountains, and the Western Carpathian Mountains. Encourage students to illustrate the regions and develop a key to show the importance of each region. Or students might prefer organizing the information into a chart such as the one on the following page.

Poland		
Region	**Location**	**Industry**
Baltic Lakes Region		
Carpathian Forelands		
Central Plains		
Coastal Lowlands		
Polish Uplands		
Sudetes Mountains		
Western Carpathian Mountains		

Ask students to think of the seven regions of Poland. Then ask them to describe which region is most like the area where they live. What are the differences?

Have students compare Poland's size to the size of their country (state, territory). Then have them compare Poland's population to the population of their country (state, territory). Explain to students that about 70 percent of Poland's people live in cities and towns. This percentage has increased significantly since World War II. Ask students to compare this population distribution with the area where they live.

Poland is about the size of the state of New Mexico in the United States. Have children check the size and population of New Mexico. With this information, have them determine which area is more densely populated. Guide students to compute percentages to compare population density.

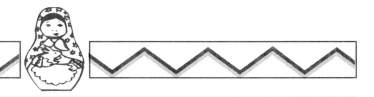

Explain to students that Poland's six largest cities are Warsaw, Lódź, Kraków, Wrocław, Poznań, and Gdańsk. Have students check the populations of each of these cities in a current encyclopedia or almanac. Have them locate cities of comparable population in their country (territory, province).

Remind students that Poland has been under the rule of several different invaders. Have interested students research how the boundaries of Poland have changed from the 1500s to the present time. Arrange students into several groups to complete eight maps of Poland showing the area of the country during the 1500s, 1600s, 1772, 1793, 1795, 1800s, 1900s, and present time. These times represent major territorial changes for the country of Poland.

Invite interested students to learn more about Lech Walesa.

Explain to students that Poles say one must always carry an umbrella because the weather can change instantly. Encourage interested students to research Poland's climate. Ask them to compare Poland's climate with the climate where they live.

Remind students that education is important to the Poles. Entrance to a university is determined by competitive examinations, and only about 5 percent of all applicants are accepted into the best schools. In Poland, a university education takes five to six years to complete. And over 60 percent of the medical and dental students in Poland are women. Discuss with students how this information about college in Poland compares to their area. Then ask students to share their thoughts on college and what they would like to study.

Discuss the gigantic salt mine that is located near Kraków in Wieliczka. Visitors to these mines can see underground rooms covered with salt crystals. There are statues carved from salt and a huge ballroom where parties are sometimes held. A popular Polish legend, Kinga's Dowry, explains how

the salt mine was made. A reproducible version of this legend is provided on page 59. Offer students a chance to enjoy the legend. Then encourage them to create a Readers' Theater script, a play, or a legend with the same story line and different characters or the same characters and a different story line. Invite interested students to learn more about Polish salt mines. Students may also be interested in researching salt mining.

Coal mining is an important industry in Poland. Explain to students that the country of Poland ranks fifth in the world behind the United States, Russia, China, and Germany in coal production. Invite interested students to research coal mining and create an interesting presentation for their classmates. Ask them to answer questions such as the following.

- **How is coal mined?**

- **How is coal shipped?**

- **What are the uses of coal?**

- **What are the dangers of coal mining?**

Warsaw, the Capital City

Have students compare the size of the city of Warsaw to the size of their city or town. Then have them compare Warsaw's population to the population of their city. From this information, discuss how students can determine which area is more densely populated.

Remind students that the laboratory where Marie Curie first began her experiments with radium is located in Warsaw. Encourage interested students to research this scientist and the work she and her husband, Pierre, accomplished.

Most of the city of Warsaw was destroyed during World War II. When the residents of Warsaw rebuilt their city, they wanted it to look as it had before the war. Discuss with students why they think the Polish people chose to make their city look as it had rather than creating modern-looking architecture. Invite students to create and describe their ideas of a beautiful city. Students may wish to write descriptions as well as draw or create models.

POLISH CULTURAL CONNECTIONS

Through the study of cultures, students can gain an understanding of and respect for diversity. The following activities can help students connect across the continents with the people in this interesting culture.

Polish Language

Official Language of Poland

Polish is the official language of Poland and the native tongue of the Poles. To a nonspeaking listener, Polish sounds a lot like Russian, but the written forms of the two languages look very different because of the alphabet used. The Polish language uses the Roman alphabet of 26 letters with a few unique letters created by adding various accent markings. Therefore, written Polish looks familiar to people whose written language uses the Roman alphabet, like English or Spanish.

To non-Polish speaking people, written Polish looks very difficult to pronounce. But the language is not nearly as difficult to pronounce as it looks because the same letters always have the same sounds. Offer students an opportunity to learn some familiar Polish words and phrases. A reproducible is provided on page 60. Or invite a Polish-speaking adult to the class to share some of his or her language with the students.

Greetings and Titles

Several forms of greetings are customary in the Polish culture. Adults will generally shake hands upon meeting. Men will sometimes kiss the extended hand of women in greeting. It is also common for close female friends to greet each other by kissing both cheeks.

While teenagers and children are addressed by their first names, only close adult friends will address each other

by using first names. In formal conversation or business, a professional person is addressed by title only. In other situations, a professional person's title is used before his or her last name. Discuss with students how their culture compares with the greetings and titles in the Polish culture.

Legends of Poland

Many, many legends have been told for centuries in Poland. One popular legend concerns how the nation of Poland began.

According to this legend, once long ago three brothers lived together in a northern land. Their names were Lech (Leh), Czech (Cheh), and Rus (Roos). All three loved their home with its rich, green land and huge trees with bright birds singing from their branches.

But after a while, the brothers found themselves with a problem. Each of them had done so well, there was no longer room enough for all of them to live there. The three brothers went for a walk to think about a solution to their problem. Lech climbed a tree to see what he could see. To the south he saw tall mountains, lush plains, and gleaming lakes and rivers. He called down to his brothers and told them what he had seen. Czech said, "I will go to the south and make my home." And he did.

Next Lech looked to the east. He saw golden grass prairies and river valleys filled with animals and birds. He called down to his brother Rus. "I will go to the east and make my home," said Rus. And he did. Then Lech looked to the north, and all he saw was the sea. He looked to the west and saw thick, dark forests filled with strange, savage tribes. "What shall I do?" he cried. "I cannot make my home in either of those places!" Then Lech stopped looking so far away. Instead he looked at the tree where he sat. Right beside him he saw an eagle's nest with three young white eagles.

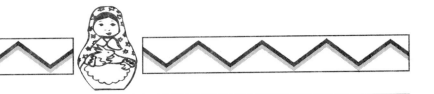

"Now I know what I must do," he said. "I will stay right here and make this my home." So Lech built a town and called it *Gniezno*, which means "nest." It became the first town in Poland. And a white eagle is a part of Poland's national coat of arms.

Discuss with students what they can learn about the Polish people from this legend. Then invite students to write their own legends to explain how their country (state, territory) began. Students may enjoy reading other Polish legends and folktales. Suggestions are provided in the bibliography beginning on page 46.

The Sea Captain

Students will enjoy hearing and/or performing this adapted Polish folktale. One version of the tale and paper-folding directions to embellish it are provided on pages 61-66.

Polish Riddles

Riddles are questions with clever or surprising answers, often involving a pun. A riddle generally asks a question by describing something in a way that at first suggests an answer other than the true one. Share with students the following riddles from Poland. Ask students what they can learn about the culture or the country from the riddles.

- A beautiful girl lost her earrings while playing in the meadow. The moon left them there, but the sun came and picked them up. (Dewdrops)

- I have neither body nor soul, but when I play on my flute, everything starts moving. (Wind)

- A quick knight walks along the stream, and when the little friends see him, they all run away. (A stork and frogs)

- There are fields beyond measure
  And cattle beyond counting;
  Horned is the shepherd,
  And rich is the landlord.
  (The sky, the stars, the moon, and the sun)

Polish Music

Frédéric Chopin

Frédéric Chopin was a musician from Poland who achieved fame throughout the world in the early 1800s. His music, almost all written for solo piano, became an inspiration for the people of his troubled country. It is described as bittersweet—both happy and sad at the same time. Explain to students that classical music, such as that composed by Chopin, is enjoyed forever as opposed to "popular" music that is more timely. Play some of Chopin's music for the students. Suggested recordings are provided in the bibliography on pages 51-52. Invite interested students to learn more about the life and music of this famous composer. A good resource is the book *Frédéric Chopin* by Richard Tames. More information on this book is provided in the bibliography on page 47.

Polish Dances

The Poles have danced and sung from the beginning of time. First there was the *polonaise*, a dance which came from the royal court. Then came the *mazurka*, which has become Poland's national dance. If possible, play an example of polonaise music and music for the mazurka. Suggested recordings are provided in the bibliography on page 52. Ask students to compare the two types of music. Have them explain what kinds of movements are suggested by the two types of music.

Singing

Throughout history, music has been very much a part of people's lives in Poland. The Poles sang as they worked. There

was a song of the mill as its wheel turned around. There was the song of the scythe as it went through wheat. There were songs that women sang as they beat their washing dry. The shepherd in the Carpathian Mountains played his long pipe to lead the sheep over the stony slopes. Discuss with students situations in their culture where music and singing play an important role.

Polish Spirit

Remind students that the Polish people have had trouble with invaders throughout history. Despite their troubles, they have always continued singing. The Polish spirit is heard in the courageous songs they have sung throughout history. A song that typifies the Polish spirit is the hymn called the *Heynal*. This hymn is played every hour from the brass bell in the tower of the Church of the Trumpeter in Kraków. The hymn ends with what the Poles refer to as the *Broken Note*. In addition, Polish radio also broadcasts the Heynal at noon each day as a symbol of the spirit of the Polish people. The following story is told about this famous hymn.

> Long ago in the year 1241, a youthful watchman was on duty in the tower of the Church of the Trumpeter. The watchman saw an army of Tartar invaders headed for Kraków. As he blew his trumpet to warn the people of Kraków, he was shot and killed by a Tartar arrow. But his warning gave the city enough time to close its gates to keep out the invaders. He was playing at the time he was shot, and the story says he tried to finish the *Heynal* before he died. But his life was taken from him before he was able to sound the last note. So to this day, the *Heynal* is ended on the Broken Note.

If possible, locate a recording of this hymn to share with the students.

Ignace Jan Paderewski

This famous Pole composed music, played the piano, and served as a statesman for his native country. Ignace Paderewski was born in 1860 and began taking piano lessons when he was six years old. By the age of eighteen, he was a professor at the Warsaw Conservatory. During World War I when Poland was being destroyed by Russian attacks and German oppression, Paderewski toured North and South America playing his music and asking for help for the people of his country. Following this war, he represented his country at the Versailles peace conference and at the League of Nations. His efforts helped Poland become an independent nation again. He gave almost all of the money he earned as a pianist to his country. Discuss with students performers from their culture who have used their talents to help their country.

Polish Art

Wooden Nesting Dolls

Poland is a country rich in folk art. Nesting dolls, which were first developed in Russia, continue to enjoy an important place in the art of Poland. Nesting dolls are often designed to represent several generations. As a group, the Polish dolls function mainly as children's toys rather than objects of art.

Polish nesting dolls are called *krakowianka*. They are made of various pine woods and spray-painted in large, flat areas of color in an overlapping style. Smaller details are hand-painted. Polish dolls are often distinguished by protruding noses on the largest dolls in the set. The Polish dolls are most often grouped in sets of three, but sets of four, five, six, and seven exist as well. The dolls are usually dressed in Polish attire from the Kraków region.

Discuss with students what doll or other toy they think is representative of their culture and why. Then students might enjoy hearing or performing the reproducible nesting doll story provided on pages 67-69.

Folk Art

Folk art is an important part of the Polish culture, and both the government and the people of Poland agree that it must be continued. In days gone by, engaging in folk art enriched the lives of rural people. Today many Polish farmers still work on their art in the winter when they cannot farm. The Polish people are experts at many folk arts including tapestry weaving, wood carving, pottery making, embroidery, and painting on glass. The Polish people seem quite fearless in the bright colors they produce and use together. Students might enjoy seeing examples of common Polish embroidery motifs. Examples are provided in the reproducible on page 70. Invite students to re-create the motifs on drawing paper and color them using bright colors.

Cepelia are special shops that have been set up to sell genuine folk art to visitors. Polish folk artists also use what they make. They might eat from pottery dishes made by an uncle and store their clothes in a chest painted in bright designs by their mother.

Ask students to describe crafts or folk art members of their families make or collect. Categorize the crafts according to whether they are designed for use or to be enjoyed as art. Encourage students to bring examples to share. If possible, invite an interested family member to demonstrate and teach his or her craft to the class.

Polish *Wycinanki:* Paper Cutouts

In the early 1800s, farming families in Poland decorated their homes with beautiful cut-paper designs called *wycinanki* (vǐ-chee-non-key). In the spring before Easter, the Poles would whitewash their walls and then glue colorful wycinanki to them for decoration. Although you would never guess it from the lacy intricacy of the designs, wycinanki were cut from the only tool available—sheep shears. The designs were also cut out freehand with no preliminary sketching. The designs were originally cut by women as the Polish men

did more of the heavy craft work such as carpentry and black-smithing. Young and old women would gather together to create the designs. The work was not done for money but to decorate the home. The wycinanki were cut from folded paper. Then when the paper was opened up and spread flat, the design was symmetrical. The subject matter reflected the Polish countryside—trees, flowers, roosters, birds, and stars. The cutouts were more decorative than realistic.

Today wycinanki are most often made to be framed or sold to people living in other cities and other countries. To this day, exhibitions and competitions are held in which people display their wycinanki. Prizes are given for originality and skill. Students might enjoy creating their own wycinanki. Reproducible directions for two forms of wycinanki are provided on pages 71 and 72.

Posters

Many Polish artists are recognized as world leaders in the field of designing posters. There is a poster museum near Warsaw where many Polish posters are displayed. Invite students to think about what they have learned about Polish culture and create a prize-winning poster inviting people to visit Poland. Remind students that posters are noted for their simplicity and clear messages.

The Arts

The Poles are very concerned about keeping the arts alive and well in their culture. Theaters, opera halls, and movie houses are supported by the government. This means these establishments have the money to try new and adventurous experiments. Government money also means that tickets are inexpensive and Polish people can go to plays, operas, and movies fairly often. Discuss with students how this is similar to or different from their culture.

Polish Education

School Day

Polish children go to school six days a week—Monday through Saturday. Their school day lasts from eight or nine in the morning until one or two in the afternoon. In some schools, students at different grades arrive at different times. Even though Polish students can go home early in the afternoon, they often remain at school until four or five in the afternoon. This is because both parents often work until later in the afternoon. In addition, there are interesting things for the students to do after school. Clubs and special classes meet during these after-school times. Students can participate in photography, cooking, skiing, making furniture, singing, or playing the violin. Students who want to study poetry, do chemistry experiments, or learn English can attend special classes held after school.

Discuss with students what special classes they would like to see held after school. Then invite students to form debate teams to discuss the advantages and disadvantages of six shorter school days and different grades attending school at different times. Once the debate has been staged, have the debaters poll the class and graph the results.

Elementary Schools

Polish elementary schools start with kindergarten and go through eighth grade. Young students in Poland study many things. When they start school, they learn how to read and write in Polish. Other subjects studied in elementary school are math, Polish history, world history, geography, biology, chemistry, physics, art, music, Polish and foreign literature, citizenship, health, cooking, and crafts. Polish areas of study are often advanced as compared to other cultures. For example, Polish students often take algebra in sixth grade! Also, all Polish elementary students take at least one foreign language—Russian, German, and English are the most common. Discuss with students common subjects studied in their schools through eighth grade. Invite an interested

group of students to create a visual to compare and contrast the subjects studied in the two cultures.

Rules and Expected Behavior for School

Polish students have many rules to follow.

- **They leave their shoes in the cloakroom in the morning. Throughout the day, they wear slippers to keep the floors clean.**
- **Polish students wear school smocks with badges with the school's name and a number. Students are most often addressed by their numbers instead of their names.**
- **Each student shares a big desk with another student.**
- **When the teacher enters the room, students are expected to stand up.**
- **Polish students assume part of the responsibility for taking care of the school and keeping it clean.**

Discuss students' reactions to the rules listed above. Then ask students how they could become more involved in taking care of their school. Encourage students to form a committee and make suggestions of ways to involve the whole school.

Secondary Schools and College

After Polish students graduate from eighth grade, they can choose from several options. Although most go on for more schooling, some young people—especially farm children—begin working right away. Others go to vocational school to learn a job for a factory or a business. After three years of vocational school, these students go to work. Other students, especially those who want to go to college, go to secondary school for four or five years.

There are two different kinds of secondary schools in Poland. One is for those who are interested in technical careers. Agricultural science, industrial engineering, and computer design are examples of technical careers. These students will

most likely continue their educations in a technical college. The other kind of high school is for students interested in the liberal arts. These students typically go to a university after they graduate and later become teachers, art historians, or astronomers.

Polish students are chosen for college based on their scores on a test taken after high school graduation. Only the highest-scoring students are chosen for each field of study. Also, a student's course of study is determined by the Polish government's economic plan. This plan determines the number of students who can study in each field in college. Due to this preplanning, students are guaranteed a position in their fields when they graduate. Polish college students do not have to pay for their college. In fact, colleges often pay the students to go to school!

Discuss with students how Poland's secondary education compares with secondary education in their culture. Encourage students to discuss the advantages and disadvantages of the policies in each culture. Invite students to share their college plans and whether they would want to attend a vocational school, technical college, or a university if they lived in Poland.

Polish Food/Cooking

Polish Meals

Poles eat four meals a day. They start the day with breakfast at home before work or school. A typical breakfast includes bread and butter and tea or coffee. Other common breakfast foods are eggs, sausage, cheese, ham or other sliced meats, and cake. Poles don't eat lunch at work or school. Instead they enjoy a "second breakfast" at ten or eleven in the morning. Second breakfast is often bread and butter with cheese, sliced cucumbers and tomatoes, and tea. The biggest meal of the day, *obiad*, is eaten between three and five o'clock in the

afternoon or early evening. It usually consists of soup, meat or fish, potatoes, vegetables, and dessert. Then later in the evening around eight or nine, Poles eat a light supper consisting of the same types of foods eaten for breakfast. Before a meal, Poles might say *Smacznego*. This means *I hope your food is delicious and you enjoy your meal.* A reproducible potato recipe that might be enjoyed for obiad is included on page 73.

Food Preferences

Poles eat veal and pork but very little beef. It would be unusual to see a Polish person eating a steak or a hamburger. Poles also do not like to drink plain water, and they don't usually put ice cubes in their drinks. Since poppies are grown in Poland, many recipes call for poppy seeds. These seeds are used in casseroles, salads, cakes, and other desserts. Discuss with students the food preferences evident in their culture.

Fruits and Vegetables

Citrus fruits do not grow in Poland. They are special treats that can be bought only a few months of the year. So most of the time Poles eat the fruits and vegetables that are grown in their country. Potatoes, beets, cabbage, spinach, apples, pears, currants, and strawberries are some of the fruits and vegetables grown and enjoyed in Poland when they are in season. Invite students to make a fruit and vegetable salad eaten in Poland. A reproducible recipe for red cabbage and apple salad is provided on page 74.

Polish Soups

Soup is very popular in Poland. But rather than spooning it out of a mug, Polish people often use a knife and fork to eat a bowl of thick Polish soup. Polish soup is made from all kinds of vegetables and even some fruits. *Barszcz* is made with beets, and *kapuszniak* is made with sauerkraut. Mushrooms, barley, peas, potatoes, and beetroot are also

used in Polish soups. In the summer, cold soup is made with fruits such as pureed strawberries, apples, cherries, blueberries, or raspberries thickened with sour cream. Reproducible recipes for barszcz and kapusniak are provided on pages 75 and 76.

Holiday Meals

The Polish people celebrate both Christmas and Easter with lots of good things to eat. Christmas and Easter dinners often include ham, sausage, and *bigos*, a stew made with sausage and sauerkraut. These holiday meals also contain many choices of soups and vegetables and plenty of little cakes. Some Polish cakes are only a little bit sweet, such as poppy seed cake, cake stuffed with cream cheese filling, and some fruit cakes. Others such as *pierniki* (honey cakes), gingerbread, rum cakes, and *pączki* (ball-shaped doughnuts filled with jelly and rolled in sugar) are much sweeter. Discuss with students when big meals are a customary part of their family celebrations and what typical meals consist of. Students might enjoy making Polish poppy seed cake. A reproducible recipe is provided on page 78.

Wigilia

Christmas Eve dinner is called the *wigilia*. Traditionally, Polish families go without food throughout Christmas Eve Day. When evening comes, they are ready for a feast. But no one can start eating until the first star appears. Polish children eagerly watch the sky to be the first to see the star. Christmas Eve dinners can include baked fish, almond soup, beet soup, noodles, cabbage, poppy seed cake, and potato dumplings. No meat is served. Several superstitions surround Christmas Eve dinner. There must be an odd number of foods, and the Poles consider it bad luck not to taste every food that is served. Also, an extra place is set at the Christmas Eve table for an unexpected guest. It is considered good luck if the place is filled with another hungry person. Invite students to fix noodles with poppy seeds, a

traditional Polish dish served only on Christmas Eve. A
reproducible recipe is provided on page 79.

Polish Holidays/Celebrations

Christmas Season

Christmas is an important holiday season in Poland. Advent is
the start of the Christmas season. Traditionally, Advent was
the time when Polish people got together for winter work parties. One person read or told stories while the others did inside
work such as repairing farm tools, spinning, or sewing.

Today the Poles celebrate several saints' days during this
time. Advent begins on November 12 with Saint Martin's
Day. Saint Nicholas Day (December 6) is an especially popular saint's day for Polish children. This is the day when Saint
Nicholas brings presents and honey cakes to all good children. In the Polish tradition, Saint Nicholas is dressed as a
bishop and arrives in a sleigh with his assistant, who helps
him give out the gifts.

After a hearty Christmas Eve dinner, Polish families enjoy
singing Christmas carols. Families often attend church on
Christmas Eve. Some Polish families open gifts on Christmas
Eve. Santa (called the Star Man in some parts of Poland) may
visit on Christmas Eve and leave more gifts for the children.
Christmas Day is usually a quiet day spent with the family.
In some homes, gifts are opened on Christmas Day rather
than Christmas Eve. The days between Christmas and New
Year's Eve are days to visit friends. New Year's Eve is called
Sylvester in Poland. Two customs connected with Sylvester
are having grand balls with music and dancing and playing
tricks on friends. The Christmas season actually continues
through the Twelfth Night (January 6) and Candlemas on
February 2, when everyone brings lighted candles to church.
Janina Domanska, a popular Polish author of children's
books, took the words of a famous Polish Christmas carol to
create a book. *Din Dan Don It's Christmas* is a beautifully

illustrated picture book students might enjoy. More information on this book is provided on page 49 of the bibliography.

Kulig

Kulig is an important winter holiday. The custom started long ago in Poland. One family would get into its sleigh covered with jingle bells and take a fast ride to the home of a neighbor. While the visit would not be planned, the visitors were always welcomed with food and drink. Then the second family would join the first family and travel on to a third friend's house. Sometimes the kulig would last for days! In Poland today, the kuligs do not last as long. And while some families in the country still travel by sleigh, families in the cities usually go by car, bus, or trolley. Discuss with students why they think this custom developed. Then ask students to explain if this custom reminds them of any similar custom within their culture and to describe it.

Easter Season

Easter is another long and important holiday in Poland. The Easter season begins with Carnival, which is a day for parties before Lent begins. Lent is the forty weekdays before Easter, and it is a time of fasting and praying for the Catholics of Poland. On Holy Saturday, the day before Easter, Poles take baskets of food to church to have them blessed. In the baskets are bread, sausage, cakes, eggs, and butter shaped into lambs. The baskets are covered with beautiful hand-embroidered napkins. This blessed food is eaten for Easter dinner. The traditional Easter main dish was a stuffed pig's head.

Poles are proud of their beautiful Easter eggs called *pisanki*. These lovely eggs have many colors and designs. Pisanki and flowers decorate the table for Easter dinner, which is a big feast for the Polish people. The pisanki process begins three weeks before Easter with the

preparation of the eggs. Since boiled eggs often crack, and blown eggs (eggs with the insides drained) do not immerse well, pisanki eggs are usually raw, simply left to dry up inside over a period of time—often up to a year. After the drying, a wax design is applied to the outside of the eggshell with a *kistka*, a pointed brass cone with a wooden handle. Beeswax is shaved into the cone of the kistka and melted over a candle. The decorator draws wax lines wherever the dye is not wanted. The egg is then dipped into a light color. More wax is applied wherever the light color is to be protected. Then darker colors are added one by one, until the last which is usually black. Offer students an opportunity to create their own pisanki. Reproducible directions are provided on page 80.

Other Common Celebrations

In addition to Mother's Day and Father's Day, people in Poland celebrate Women's Day in early March and Children's Day in early June. For Women's Day, men and children give gifts of candy and flowers to women friends, relatives, and teachers. Children are rewarded with presents, a special trip, or some favorite food for Children's Day.

Świętojanki or *Sobótka* (Saint John's Eve) is a Polish holiday observed on June 23. During the day, there are big outdoor picnics. After sundown, the young people of Poland practice a romantic custom. Single girls and women place wreaths of flowers and lighted candles on tiny rafts. The rafts are placed in a stream to float by young men standing by the water. If a man wades into the water and catches the raft of a woman he's interested in, it means good luck for their love. If he can catch the raft without the candle going out, it means they will get married soon! Harvest festivals are common in late summer and early fall. Our Lady of the Harvest takes place on August 15. In the country, Poles wear native costumes and wreaths made out of wheat or other grains.

Hallows' Eve is on October 31. At this time, some Polish people visit cemeteries, light candles, and place food on the graves of their ancestors. All Saints' Day is observed on

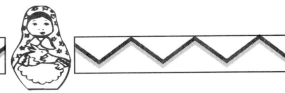

November 1. On this day, Poles visit and decorate the graves of relatives and friends who have died. Discuss with students holidays celebrated in their culture that are similar to those listed above. Encourage interested students to create Venn diagrams or other visuals to compare and contrast Polish customs and holidays with those of their culture.

Name Day

Name Day occurs every day on the Polish calendar. In Poland, each day honors a different saint. The Polish people who share the same first name as that saint are also honored. For example, on Saint Barbara's Day, all Barbaras celebrate.

In Poland, a person's name is much more important than his or her birthday. Children do celebrate their birthdays by bringing cake and candy to school to share, but older children and adults have birthday celebrations on their name days instead. There are presents, cakes, and other good food. Discuss with students the advantages and disadvantages of this Polish custom.

Polish Recreation

Soccer and Volleyball

While Polish young people enjoy playing basketball and volleyball, their most popular team sport is soccer. Soccer is called football in Europe. In Poland, soccer is played by schoolchildren all the way up to professional soccer players. Poles enjoy playing and watching this sport. Whether watching the game on television or in one of the stadiums, the Polish people become very involved. The Polish soccer team won the gold medal at the Olympics in Munich in 1972 and the silver medal at the Olympics in Montreal in 1976.

Poland is also known for producing champion volleyball teams. Its teams brought home gold medals for volleyball from the world competition in Mexico in 1974 and again at the 1976 Montreal Olympics. Invite students who play soccer or volleyball to demonstrate the game. Or invite a coach or college or professional player to teach the students about the game.

Winter Sports

Skiing and other winter sports are popular in Poland, especially in the rugged Tatra Mountains. Poles, as well as vacationers from other countries, enjoy staying at resorts in mountain towns such as the one near Zakopane. Children often join skiing clubs at school to learn the sport. Throughout Poland, adults and children enjoy sledding and ice skating. Sometimes children bring sleds or skates to school to use at recess. Polish children enjoy ice hockey and figure skating on rinks throughout the country. Invite children to discuss winter sports they enjoy, if appropriate. Then encourage students to create a mural of winter sports.

Medalists and World-Record Setters

Although many Poles play games or sports for enjoyment, many serious Poles have gone on to become medalists and world-record holders. Invite interested students to learn more about the following famous Polish athletes.

Track and Field

Wladysław Kozakiewicz

Stella Walsh

Grażyna Rabsztyn

Skiing

Wojciech Fortuna

Andrzej Bachleda

Gliding

Ryszard Makula

Wrestling

Stanisław Cyganiewicz (also known as Zbysko)

Krystyna Chojnowska-Liskiewicz

Krystyna Chojnowska-Liskiewicz was the first woman to sail around the world alone. She spent two years and twenty-four days (from March 1976 to April 1978) accomplishing this feat. Her vessel was a thirty-two foot sailboat she named *Mazurek*. Her route started at the Canary Islands (off the African coast near Spain) past South America, Africa, and Australia, and back to the Canary Islands.

Her voyage was not without hardship. At one point, she became so sick she had to spend three weeks in a hospital. Another time she was almost hit by a freighter near the Panama Canal. Invite students to trace her route on a world map, calculate the miles traveled, and estimate average miles traveled per day.

Recreational Sports

Most Polish workers have four weeks of vacation a year. Because of this, Polish families can take long vacations together. Because of the small size of Poland, it is possible to get anywhere in the country by car, bus, or train within a day or two.

There are many kinds of countryside for people with different interests including lakes, mountains, seacoast, forests, and even a small desert near Kraków. During summer, vacationers enjoy hiking and rafting in the mountain streams. In the forests, there are national parks with specially protected areas for birds and animals. Sailboating, canoeing, yachting, fishing, and camping are

popular pastimes at the many lakes. Along the Baltic Sea, Poles enjoy swimming, sunbathing, and taking boat trips to other small islands not far from the coast.

Discuss with students areas of their country they have visited with their families and what types of recreation they enjoyed.

POLISH CULTURAL EXTENSIONS

There is so much more to learn about Poland. Select from the topics suggested below, or choose your own topics to add to your growing understanding and knowledge of Poland.

- Do further research on any of the cultural information presented. For instance, learn more about the Polish language, music, clothing, food/cooking, holidays/celebrations, or recreation.

- Learn more about the native plant or animal life in a region of this country. Small animals, insects, and plants often play major roles in defining a culture.

- Do further research on the geography of Poland.

- Find articles in the daily newspaper dealing with persons, places, or things in Poland.

- Learn more about rural life versus city life in this country.

- Study Poland's involvement in World War II.

- Learn more about the Polish government and what recent changes it has undergone.

- Investigate the economic history of Poland.

- Research the history of Communism and its fall in Poland.

- Research Polish currency and its exchange rate (zloty and groszy).

- Study the life and discoveries of Nicholas Copernicus, the Father of Astronomy.

- Choose one of the following people to research. Determine why the person figures prominently in the history of Poland.

    Alfred Nobel

    Marie Curie

    Wladysław Stanisław Reymont

    Henryk Sienkiewicz

    Ignacy Lukasziewicz

- Research how Thaddeus Kościuszko and Casimir Pulaski figure into both the history of the United States and the history of Poland.

- Find out how Helena Modjeska represented her native country of Poland.

- Study Poland's native dress. Create an interesting, colorful display.

- Plan a visit to Poland. Check on airline fares; passports, visas, or other entry requirements; currency; where to stay; interesting places to visit; and so on.

- Amber is a substance that is sometimes washed up on the shores of Poland on the Baltic Sea. Find out more about amber.

- Read another book on Poland. Ask your teacher for suggestions. Present a report on your reading.

- Correspond with a pen pal in Poland. Write to the following address for more information.

Embassy of Poland
2224 Wyoming Avenue
Washington, DC 20008

ANNOTATED BIBLIOGRAPHY

Books

Babushka retold by Charles Mikolaycak. Readers will enjoy this retelling of the classic Christmas story about Babushka, the Russian peasant woman who was invited by the three Wise Men to visit baby Jesus. Holiday House, 1984. [Picture Book]

Call Me Ruth by Marilyn Sachs. This is a warm and moving story about the struggles of a young girl who comes to New York City from Russia with her family at the turn of the century. Doubleday, 1982. [Middle Grades]

Chicken Sunday by Patricia Polacco. When her own Babushka dies, a young girl adopts her black friend's grandmother, Miss Eula, to take her place. Putnam, 1992. [Picture Book]

Children Are Children Are Children by Ann Cole. This book explores the cultures of several Eastern European countries. Little, 1978. [Middle Grades]

A Day of Pleasure: Stories of a Boy Growing Up in Warsaw by Isaac Bashevis Singer. This author tells nineteen stories about his boyhood in Warsaw, Poland. Farrar, 1986. [Middle Grades]

The Devil's Arithmetic by Jane Yolen. This book is a frightening and stirring account of life in a Nazi concentration camp in Poland in 1942. Puffin, 1990. [Middle Grades]

Ellis Island: Gateway to the New World by Leonard Everett Fisher. Authentic photographs and interesting information bring to life the history of this great landmark. Holiday House, 1986. [Middle Grades]

Frédéric Chopin by Richard Tames. This interesting, easily read book explains the life of this famous musician. Watts, 1991. [Middle Grades]

Here Comes the Cat by Vladimir Vagin and Frank Asch. Throughout this book, a mouse rides his bike through various scenes warning about the approach of the cat. Scholastic, 1989. [Picture Book]

The Hundred Dresses by Eleanor Estes. The little Polish girl in this book teaches her classmates a lesson. Harcourt, 1974. [Middle Grades]

Immigrant Girl: Becky of Eldridge Street by Brett Harvey. Life is different for Becky and her family when they move from Russia to New York in 1910. Holiday House, 1987. [Picture Book]

The Island on Bird Street by Uri Orlev. During World War II, a Jewish boy is left on his own in a ruined house in the Warsaw Ghetto. Houghton, 1992. [Middle Grades]

The Keeping Quilt by Patricia Polacco. This is the story of Great Gramma Anna, who came from Russia, and the quilt that is passed down through the generations. Simon, 1988. [Picture Book]

The Land and People of Poland by Eric P. Kelly. This book introduces the reader to the land and people of Poland. Lippincott, 1972. [Middle Grades]

The Man from the Other Side by Uri Orlev. This is the story of Marek, a young boy living just outside the Warsaw ghetto during World War II. Houghton, 1991. [Middle Grades]

Max and Sally and the Phenomenal Phone by Milos Macourek. This is an attractively illustrated picture book about a magic phone. It was first published in Czechoslovakia. Wellington, 1989. [Picture Book]

Molly's Pilgrim by Barbara Cohen. Molly is embarrassed by her old-country clothes and imperfect English, and she wants to return to Russia. Lothrop, 1983. [Picture Book]

Mrs. Katz and Tush by Patricia Polacco. Mrs. Katz is a Polish-Jewish immigrant who is lonely now that her husband Myron has died. Bantam, 1992. [Picture Book]

My Grandmother's Journey by John Cech. The author based this beautiful and simply written book on his grandmother's own journey from Russia after World War II. Bradbury, 1991. [Picture Book]

Night Journey by Kathryn Lasky. Rachel's ailing great-grandmother tells about her childhood in Russia. Puffin, 1986. [Middle Grades]

Poland, Land of Freedom Fighters by Christine Pfeiffer. This is a thorough and interesting presentation of life in Poland. Dillon, 1984. [Middle Grades]

Poland, Places in the News by Gail B. Stewart. This is an easy-to-read book on the past and present political situation in Poland. Crestwood House, 1990. [Middle Grades]

The Pup Grew Up by Samuel Marshak. Readers will enjoy this amusing story about a missing dog and the substitution that was attempted. Mr. Marshak is a famous children's author in Russia. Holt, 1989. [Picture Book]

The Trumpeter of Kraków by Eric Kelly. This mystery story is centered on an attack on the ancient city of Kraków in medieval Poland. Macmillan, 1992. [Middle Grades]

Watch the Stars Come Out by Riki Levinson. This is a beautifully illustrated story of a young girl's trip from her homeland to join her parents in America. Dutton, 1985. [Picture Book]

Yossel Zissel and the Wisdom of Chelm by Amy Schwartz. Readers will enjoy Yossel's unique method of investing the bags of gold inherited from his Warsaw uncle. Jewish Publication Society, 1986. [Middle Grades]

Folktales

Baba Yaga by Ernest Small and Blair Lent. A nasty witch who supposedly eats bad children is the main character in this Russian folktale. Houghton, 1966. [Picture Book]

Baboushka and the Three Kings by Ruth Robbins. In this Russian folktale, an old woman endlessly searches for the Christ child. Houghton, 1986. [Picture Book]

The Best of the Bargain by Janina Domanska. This is the Polish folktale of shrewd Hugo, the hedgehog, and Olek, the not-so-clever fox. Greenwillow, 1977. [Picture Book]

Busy Monday Morning by Janina Domanska. This is a remarkable dramatization of a Polish folk song that celebrates the days of the week. Greenwillow, 1985. [Picture Book]

Din Dan Don It's Christmas by Janina Domanska. Text and pictures depict a popular Polish Christmas carol. Greenwillow, 1975. [Picture Book]

Fairy Tales from Eastern Europe by Neil Philip. These stories reflect a shared cultural heritage of the Eastern European countries represented. Houghton, 1991. [Middle Grades]

Favorite Fairy Tales Told in Poland retold by Virginia Haviland. This is a collection of six favorite fairy tales from Poland. Little, 1963. [Middle Grades]

King Krakus and the Dragon by Janina Domanska. This is a beautifully illustrated version of the famous legend about Kraków. Greenwillow, 1979. [Picture Book]

The Mitten retold by Alvin Tresselt. In this retelling of a famous Ukranian folktale, many forest animals find refuge from the cold weather in a lost mitten. Morrow, 1989. [Picture Book]

More Wise Men of Helm and Their Merry Tales by Solomon Simon. These silly Eastern European folktales take place in imaginary Helm, Poland. Behrman, 1979. [Middle Grades]

Naftali the Storyteller and His Horse, Sus, and Other Stories by Isaac Bashevis Singer. This is a collection of folktales for children, many of which take place in the imaginary Polish village of Helm. Farrar, 1987. [Middle Grades]

Pig and Bear by Vit Horejs. Pig and Bear are lovably foolish characters in this Czechoslovakian traditional tale. Four Winds, 1989. [Picture Book]

The Rumor of Pavel & Paali: A Ukranian Folktale by Carole Kismaric. This is a picture-book folktale of unusual power about twin brothers who live on the Great Plain. Harper, 1988. [Picture Book]

Scarecrow by Vladimir Zheleznikov. This is a powerful story about the struggle of the individual against the group by a noted writer for children in the Soviet Union. Harper, 1990. [Middle Grades]

The Singing Sack by Helen East. This book presents twenty-eight story songs from around the world. Sheridan, 1991. [Middle Grades]

Stories for Children by Isaac Bashevis Singer. This anthology contains folklore and biographical pieces about life in Warsaw. Farrar, 1984. [Picture Book]

The Story Vine by Anne Pellowski. Readers will enjoy these easy-to-tell stories from around the world. Macmillan, 1984. [Middle Grades]

The Treasure by Uri Shulevitz. In this Eastern European folktale, poor old Isaac travels far to seek riches. Farrar, 1986. [Picture Book]

Twelve Iron Sandals and Other Czechoslovak Tales by Vit Horejs. These traditional Czechoslovakian tales are told by a native author. Four Winds, 1989. [Middle Grades]

When Shlemiel Went to Warsaw and Other Stories by Isaac Bashevis Singer. Eight stories, some based on traditional Jewish tales, are told by one of the great storytellers. Farrar, 1986. [Middle Grades]

The Wise Men of Helm and Their Merry Tales by Solomon Simon. These silly Eastern European folktales take place in imaginary Helm, Poland. Behrman, 1942. [Middle Grades]

Zlateh the Goat and Other Stories by Isaac Bashevis Singer. This is a collection of Eastern European folktales. Harper, 1984. [Middle Grades]

Teacher References

A Collector's Guide to Nesting Dolls by Michele Lyons Lefkovitz. This book provides a comprehensive history and description of nesting dolls found throughout the world. Photographs of hundreds of doll sets are provided. Books Americana, 1989.

The Family Storytelling Book by Anne Pellowski. Traditional stories are presented with clever ideas for sharing. Macmillan, 1987.

Polish Recordings

Chopin—The Complete Preludes. Phillips, 1974.

Chopin—Concertos 1 and 2. Sony Music, 1990.

Chopin: Grand Fantasy on Polish Airs. RCA Red Label, 1969.

Chopin—Mazurkas. RCA, 1957.

Chopin—24 Preludes. Moss Music, 1988.

Polish Folk Songs and Dances. Folkways Records, 1954.

Van Cliburn—My Favorite Chopin. RCA Victor, 1961.

The Country

Poland or *Polska* (as the Poles call it) is a large country in central Europe. It is bordered by the Baltic Sea and Sweden on the north, Russia on the east, Czechoslovakia on the south, and Germany on the west. Poland is named for one of the earliest peoples to inhabit the land, the Polane tribe. Their name came from a word that means "people who live in the fields," and Poland is a land of gently rolling plains and fertile fields. It is also a land with a rich culture and history.

The Land

Poland covers approximately 120,000 square miles. The country can be divided into seven land areas: the Baltic Lakes Region, the Carpathian Forelands, the Central Plains, the Coastal Lowlands, the Polish Uplands, the Sudetes Mountains, and the Western Carpathian Mountains. While several of these areas share similar climate and geography, each has at least one distinct feature that sets it apart.

The Baltic Lakes Region covers much of northern Poland. This area contains thousands of small lakes, as well as thick forests and peat bogs. Lumbering is the area's main industry. It is also a popular vacation spot, with many opportunities for camping and hiking.

The Carpathian Forelands are located between the Vistula and San Rivers in the southern part of Poland. Kraków, a major manufacturing center, lies in the Forelands. It contains many of the country's steel mills and other heavy industry.

The Central Plains stretch across much of central Poland. This is the country's largest agricultural area. Farmers raise potatoes, rye, and sugar beets. This region is also home to the country's largest cities, including Warsaw, the capital.

The Coastal Lowlands lie along the Baltic coast. They contain sandy beaches and natural harbors that support the port cities of Gdańsk, Gdynia, and Szczecin.

The Polish Uplands is an area of rolling hills and low mountains. This area is densely populated and contains both great mineral wealth and tracts of rich farmland.

The Sudetes Mountains lie in the southwest. Forests cover these low mountain ranges. Cropland and pastures lie in the valleys and foothills of this area.

The Western Carpathian Mountains contain the steepest peaks in the country, including Rysy Peak, which towers 8,199 feet above sea level. This rugged and beautiful area is home to several national parks.

History

The first people to inhabit what is now Poland were Slavic tribes. These tribes were nomads who lived mostly by hunting and gathering. By the eighth century A.D., these tribes had united under the Polane, one of the largest groups in the area, and the Polish people came into being. Descendants of the Polane leaders ruled Poland until 1572.

Poland is in a central location and has no natural boundaries separating it from its neighbors to the east and west. As a result, Poland has always been a target for invaders. Over the years, the country has been under the control of Russia, Austria, Prussia, and Sweden. After World War I, Poland enjoyed a brief period of self-rule. However, shortly before World War II, Russia and Nazi Germany secretly agreed to partition Poland. In an attempt to maintain its independence, Poland signed a treaty with Britain and France. Both countries pledged to protect Poland if hostile forces invaded. In September 1939, German troops attacked. As a result, Britain and France declared war on Germany, and World War II began.

Exiled Polish leaders hoped to establish a democratic government after World War II ended. But the Soviet Union took control of Poland, and a Communist committee took over the government. The Polish people fought for the right to govern themselves. Many leaders, such as labor organizer Lech Walesa, were jailed or exiled. Finally, after decades of repression, the Soviet-backed government fell from power. Today Poland is attempting to develop a democratic form of government. The political situation in Poland has been changing rapidly in the past few years. Refer to current publications such as magazines for updated information.

People

The Polish people are proud of their country and its heritage. Ninety-eight percent of the people are Poles and are descended from slavic tribes that settled in the area thousands of years ago.

At one time, Poland ruled an empire that stretched across much of central Europe. Art and literature flourished during this Golden Age. Scholars from all over the world came to study at the University of Kraków. Skilled builders and artists created beautiful churches and monasteries.

Art, religion, and learning are still important in Polish life today. Artists such as painter Jan Matejko, composer Frédéric Chopin, and writer Władysław Reymont are honored for their contributions to the arts. Chopin festivals, art exhibitions, and jazz festivals are held in nearly every major city. Polish people love to dance, and folk dances are held in every village square. In addition to the work of formally trained artists, Poland is rich in folk art. Local craftspeople produce beautiful painted furniture, wood carvings, embroidered linen, and pottery.

Despite the former government's best efforts, Catholicism is still an important aspect of daily life. Most of the country's 37 million citizens are Catholics. Religious holidays such as Christmas and Easter are still celebrated with lavish pageantry.

Home and family life are also important to the Polish people. Weddings and other family gatherings are joyous events. Wedding celebrations can last up to a week, with relatives coming from hundreds of miles away. Wedding processions are still a common sight in many small towns, with participants dressed in traditional peasant costumes.

Poland's schools and universities are some of the finest in eastern Europe. Poland's literacy rate is almost 98 percent. Education through the university level is free in Poland. Children are required to attend school from ages 7 to 15. Then students who pass entrance exams go on to vocational schools or four-year secondary schools. Secondary school graduates must pass entrance exams to enter one of Poland's 10 universities. These university students follow in the footsteps of such famous Polish scientists as Marie Curie and Nicholas Copernicus.

Economy

Poland is one of the most industrialized nations in eastern Europe. Only Russia produces more manufactured goods. This is especially impressive considering that Poland's economy was once almost totally agricultural. After World War II, the government promoted the development of industry. New industrial areas were created near Warsaw, Kraków, and Gdańsk. Today nearly 40 percent of all Polish workers are employed in factories. Manufactured goods include steel, machinery, chemicals, and textiles. Poland's trading partners include Russia, Germany, Czechoslovakia, and Great Britain. Trade and industry give the Poles a higher standard of living than residents of many other Eastern European countries.

Poland has significant deposits of several important minerals. The giant coal fields in the southern part of the country produce nearly 200 million tons of coal each year. Workers also mine copper, lead, silver, and zinc. In addition, Poland has one of the world's largest underground salt mines still in operation near Wieliczka. It produces 700 tons of salt a day.

Poland's farmland is another vital resource. Most farmland in Poland is privately owned, and many farms have been owned by the same family for generations. The Uplands contain large areas of farmland with crops of potatoes, rye, sugar beets, and wheat. Hogs are also raised on these farms. In the hill country of the south, farmers raise cattle and sheep. In the north, lumber is harvested and turned into furniture and building materials.

Plants and Animals

Poland's varied landscape supports a wide variety of plants and animals. Much of the land is still forested, with hardwoods such as oak and elm and evergreens such as firs, spruce, and pine. This forested area also produces wild strawberries, raspberries, and blackberries, as well as various types of nuts and many varieties of wild mushrooms. Animals common to these wooded areas include European bison (distant cousins to the American buffalo), elks, lynx, bears, tarpans (a breed of wild pony), and foxes. In the mountain ranges, wild boars, wolves, eagles, and mountain deer roam free. Many of these animals are protected by law and inhabit natural reserves set aside for them. The Polish government has established 450 of these reserves.

Poland is blessed with an abundance of clear lakes and streams. These areas are home to many types of fish and wild fowl, including trout, several species of ducks, wild swans, and black storks. Ferns, grasses, and wild flowers such as edelweiss flourish near the lakes and rivers.

Warsaw, Poland's capital, has more than one and a half million residents. It is divided into two parts by the Vistula River. The portion of the city on the right bank is called Praga. The portion of Warsaw on the left bank of the river is divided into New Town and Old Town. Contrary to their names, both sections of the city are quite new. During World War II, almost 90 percent of Warsaw's buildings were destroyed. Thousands of people, including most of the inhabitants of Warsaw's Jewish ghetto, were killed resisting the Nazis. After the war, residents were determined to rebuild their city. Using old plans and photos, they rebuilt the Old Town's buildings almost to the last detail.

The people of Warsaw work at a variety of jobs. The central government employs thousands of workers, as does the transportation industry. Warsaw is home to both Poland's rail system and its major airline. Many Warsaw residents are employed in local factories. Tourism is also becoming an important part of the city's economy. Warsaw is also a center of education, being the home of the University of Warsaw and the Polish Academy of Science.

Warsaw is rich in historical monuments, including the fourteenth-century Cathedral of St. John, the Royal Castle, Chopin's home, and the laboratory where Marie Curie first began her experiments with radium. Another popular attraction is Lazienki Park. It is famous for its swans and lovely walking paths. Open-air markets and sidewalk cafes also lend charm to Warsaw's streets. Most residents live in small apartments and do much of their socializing at the cafes.

A wedding was being planned. The Hungarian princess Kinga was preparing to be married to the prince of Poland. Her father came to her with a question. He began by explaining that a dowry was an expensive present the bride's family gives to the groom. "What would you like for your dowry?" he then asked. Kinga thought for a minute before she said, "I want a salt mine."

Now a salt mine may sound like a very strange dowry. But long ago, salt was very valuable because it was the only way people could keep their food fresh. Unfortunately, the king could not answer his daughter's request. He had no salt mine to give.

When Kinga arrived in Poland for the wedding, she repeated her request to the Polish people. "We used to have a very small salt mine at Wieliczka," they said. "But there is no salt in it now."

Kinga asked the people to take her where the salt mine had once been. Once they arrived, she stared down the mine shaft. To everyone's surprise, she dropped her engagement ring down the mine shaft. Then she instructed the people to dig and promised a reward to the person who could find her ring.

Immediately, the people started to dig. And as they dug, they found more salt than they knew what to do with! They brought Kinga a big chunk of salt with her ring inside. Kinga was very happy to have her dowry at last!

POLISH PHRASES AND TITLES

English Word	Polish Word	Pronunciation
good morning or good afternoon	dzień dobry	jean duh´-bree
good evening	dobry wieczór	duh´-bree vyeh´-choor
good-bye	do widzenia	duh veed-zehn´-yuh
yes	tak	tahk
no	nie	ñeh
please	prosz	pro´-sheh
thank you	dziekuj	dzhehn-koo-yeh
you're welcome	prosz ę	praw-shuh
excuse me	przepraszam	pzheh-prah´-shahm
good night	dobranoc	duh-brah´-nawts
I am	jestem	yehs´-tehm
you are	jesteś	yehs´-tesh
Mr.	pan	pahn
Mrs., Miss, Ms.	pani	pah´-nee

POLISH ADJECTIVES

English Word	Male Form	Female Form
good	dobry (duh´-bri)	dobra (duh´-brah)
bad	żły (zhwih)	żla (zhwah)

happy	szcz sliwy
	  (sh-chehns-lee´-vih)
		szcz sliwa
		  (sh-chehns-lee´-vah)

sad	smutny (smoot´-nih)	smutna (smoot´-nah)
smart	m dry (mawn´-drih)	m dra (mawn´-drah)
stupid	głupi (gwoo´-pee)	głupa (gwoo´-pah)
big	duży (doo´-zhih)	duża (doo´-zhah)
small	mały (mah´-wih)	mała (mah´-wah)

Procedure and Story

There was once a young Polish man who was not satisfied with his life.

Begin with the first folded double sheet. Place it in front of you with fold at top. Bring two upper corners down to middle so they meet evenly. Press folds down.

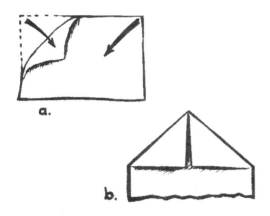

Materials

sheets of newspaper cut to the following sizes:

1 folded double sheet—cut bottom off so it is 18" x 28" (folded to 18" x 14")
2 strips each 14" long and 4½" wide, folded over to 7"x 4½"
1 strip 23" long and 6" to 7" wide
1 single sheet—cut approximately 9" off bottom, leaving a square
2 single sheets—folded down so each half is about 13½" x 11½"
scissors
pencil
marking pen

He had studied at the university and he had learned much. But he wasn't happy with his life.

Fold up upper layer of bottom flap so it meets bottom edge of triangle. Then fold it up again so it covers bottom edge. Turn figure over.

So he sat around with his friends playing cards and otherwise not doing much of anything.

Fold each side toward center so they meet. Then fold down top triangle and tuck it under the folded-over sides.

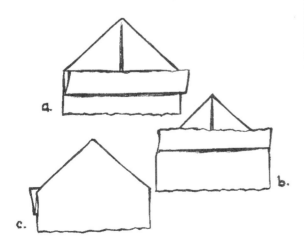

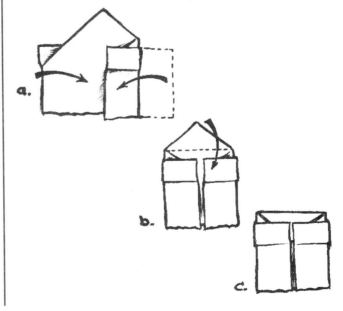

Fold in outer bottom corners so they meet in center. Fold up bottom point and tuck it behind band, but in front of folded-down upper triangle.

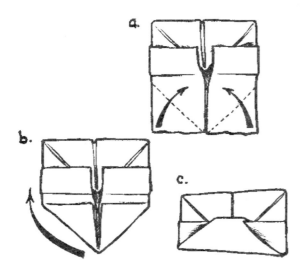

Even though he wasn't happy with his life, he always dressed in his best clothes when he went out.

Stand the figure on its crown and gently press in on the ends. Two triangles will appear on the ends, Crease the four corners to form a square base. Turn figure over and set to one side.

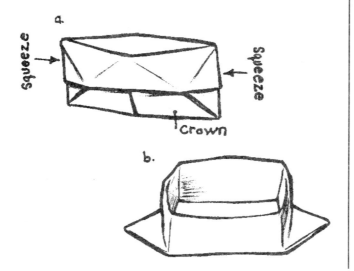

On his head, he wore a four-cornered hat.

Take up one of the 7" x 4" strips and fold the outer corners of the folded edge so they meet in the middle, making a triangle. Then fold up both layers of bottom edge so they just barely cover bottom edge of triangle. Now fold down the triangle. Press very hard on this last fold. Repeat the process for the second strip.

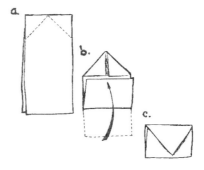

It looked like the hats students wear when they graduate from school.

Pick up the main figure. Place the flap of one folded strip behind the band with the triangle pointing out. Place flap of other strip on opposite side with triangle pointing out. The result will be a hat that looks like a mortarboard.

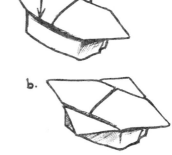

Then roll the 6" wide strip over a pencil. Let the pencil fall out and flatten one end of the tube. Cut a slit down the center of the flattened end. Cut as many additional slits as possible.

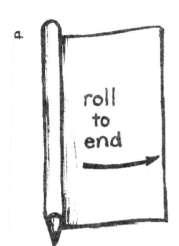

a.

roll
to
end

b.

He always wore a peacock feather in one corner of his hat.

Pull out center layer of cut strips until you have a feather-like stalk. Tuck it in one corner of the hat.

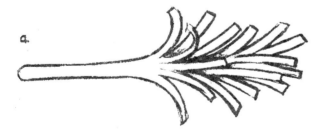

a.

b.

But the young man was bored. He liked the outdoor life and the wide-open spaces. He decided to ask his younger sister's advice. "I think you should become a sailor," the younger sister suggested to her brother.

Take single sheet that is square-sized. Find the center point by folding horizontally, opening out, then folding vertically. Then fold all four corners to center point.

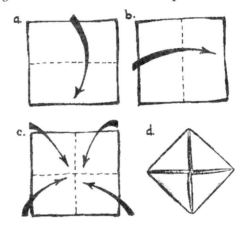

a.   b.

c.   d.

"Good idea," thought the young man. He said good-bye to his younger sister and little brother and headed for a seaport.

Turn the figure over and again fold all four corners to the center point.

a.   b.

Now open up figure and fold diagonally both ways. Shape the figure so it looks like a square table covered with a tablecloth. The four corners will each stick out to a point like a cloth hanging from a table.

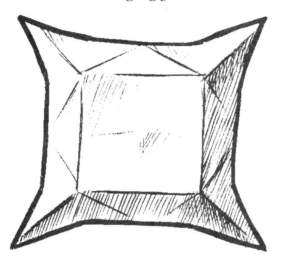

At the seaport, he saw boats and ships of many kinds, but only one that pleased him. It was a fine sailing ship. He signed up to go on a long voyage.

Fold the corner points to the sides of the square. Flatten the figure so you end up with a pinwheel shape.

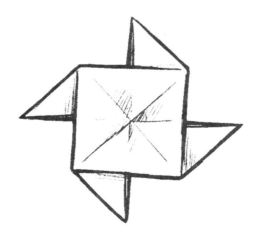

Now fold the figure in half diagonally. Fold down the two outside triangles. Turn the figure. It should look like a sailboat with a rudder. Fold the rudder behind the boat. You now have a sailboat.

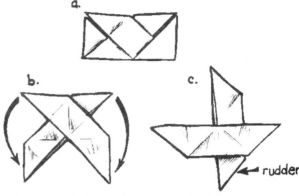

They sailed all the way to Mexico. The young man liked it there. At the end of the voyage, the captain had good news for the young man. "You are such a fine navigator," he said. "I am going to make you captain of your own ship."

Take first folded-down single sheet. With fold at the top, bring upper corners to the middle so they meet exactly. Fold down. Fold the top layer of lower flap halfway up. Fold up again and tuck the ends behind the triangle. Turn the figure over. Repeat two folds on lower flap.

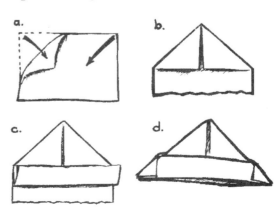

Open triangle and bring A to B and flatten out to make a square. Fold up each triangle to the top corner. Open out and you have the captain's hat.

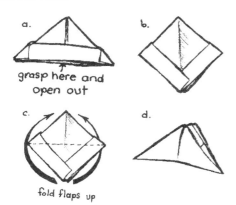

So the young man headed back to the seaport. When he arrived, it was not another sailing ship that awaited him, but a big steamship with a funnel.

Take the second folded-over single sheet. Repeat all folds as for captain's hat. Now gently open up the hat until A reaches B. Do not press down the folds of the resulting new square; instead, grasp C and D and pull apart. You will get a steamship with a funnel.

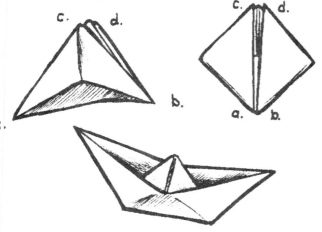

He guided his ship into the sea and was on his way. He was a good captain, but his luck was bad. One dark night, the ship collided with an iceberg. A big chunk was torn from the bow of the ship.

Take firm hold of the steamship figure and tear off the bow.

The bump sent the ship backward where it hit another iceberg. A huge chunk of the stern was torn off.

Turn the ship around and tear off the other end piece (the stern).

This was too much for the ship's steam engine. The boiler burst and the funnel blew its top.

Tear off the top of the funnel.

The ship started to sink. The captain ordered all of his crew into lifeboats. But he refused to leave the ship until everyone else was off and safe. The ship sank, and the captain found himself in the icy cold water. "Now I'm finished," he thought.

As the captain was floundering in the sea, he saw a life vest floating in front of him. He put on the life vest and floated safely to the shore. After that, he never sailed again. And never again was he bored.

Open out torn-up steamship. You will have a life vest.

There was once a man named Krak. He traveled from town to town tricking people. One day, Krak set off down a road he'd never traveled before. In the distance, he saw a town. When he came to the edge of town, he saw a young girl standing in front of her house.

Show nesting doll set closed up.

Krak could tell right away that she would be easy to trick. "Good day, miss. Where is your father?" Krak asked.

"Good day, sir," she answered sweetly. "My father is busy making many out of few."

Krak didn't understand her answer, but he didn't say so. And he worked hard not to show his puzzlement. Before he could say anymore, out from behind the girl stepped her younger sister.

Quickly reveal the second doll. Put the biggest doll together and set it aside.

Materials
a set of four nesting dolls

"Good day, young lady," said Krak. "Where is your mother?"

The second girl answered politely.

"Good day to you, sir," she said. "My mother is busy. She is busy making something better out of something good."

Krak was puzzled. Why were these sweet girls giving such mysterious answers to his questions?

At that moment, from behind the second girl stepped another younger sister. "Good day to you, young lady! Where is your brother?" said Krak.

Take off second largest doll to reveal the third doll. Put the second doll together and set it next to the biggest doll.

"Good day, sir," the third girl replied courteously. "My brother is busy. He is busy closing the door to keep it open."

"These girls are all answering me with riddles," said Krak to himself. He was ready to turn and move on to another house in the town. At that moment, from behind the third girl stepped the baby of the family.

Take apart the third doll to reveal the fourth. Set the third doll next to the first two dolls.

Krak stared at the small girl. She was hardly more than a baby. "Hello there, my sweet little one," said Krak. "Where is your grand-mother?"

"Gramma is busy," said the littlest girl. "She is busy churning butter we already spread."

That was too much for Krak. He exploded. "That's enough lies," he screamed. "You are all telling me lies!"

Hold the smallest doll.

"Oh, no, sir!" cried the baby. "We are telling you the truth."

Krak stared in disbelief. "But how can your grandmother churn but-ter you have already spread?" he asked.

The little girl explained. "Yesterday, Gramma saw that we had no more butter in the house. So she sent us to the neighbors to borrow some. And now she is churning cream into butter to return for the butter we borrowed. So she is churning butter that we already spread," she said.

"I could have figured that out if I'd only given myself time," thought Krak. He decided to find out what the other girls meant by their answers.

Put down the smallest doll and pick up the third doll.

"Now, where is your brother again?" he asked.

"He's busy closing the door to keep it open," said the next smallest girl. "See over there," she said. She pointed to a spot by the river. "My brother is mending the fish net where we keep the fish we hope to eat. When there is a hole in the net, it is like a door letting out the other fish. So my brother is closing the door. But he can't close it up too tightly because then the fish couldn't swim and breathe. So my brother is closing the door in the fish net just enough to keep it open."

"Well, I've never heard the like," thought Krak. He went to the next girl. "What was that about your mother?" he asked.

Put down the third doll and pick up the second.

"She is making something better out of something good," said the girl.

"Mother is in the kitchen. She has good flour, good eggs, and good milk. She is baking a cake. Mother is making something better out of something good. And I can't wait to have some!" she said.

"I could have figured that out," thought Krak. He approached the last girl. "What was that you said about your father?" he asked.

Put down second doll and pick up first.

"He's busy making many out of few," she said. "Listen," she continued. "Can you hear that?"

Krak listened carefully. Then he heard it. Far off he could hear the sound of an ax.

"Father is way out there in the forest." She pointed. "He is chopping wood. For every tree, we will get lots of firewood. He is making many out of few," she said.

Put down the first doll and point to all four of them.

Krak was worried. If the children of the town were this clever, what must the adults be like? "I don't think I can trick anyone here," he thought. Krak turned and walked off in the opposite direction and never came back. And that is how four clever girls kept their town from being tricked by Krak.

Point to all four of the dolls.

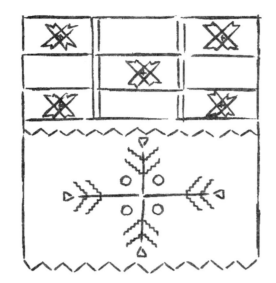

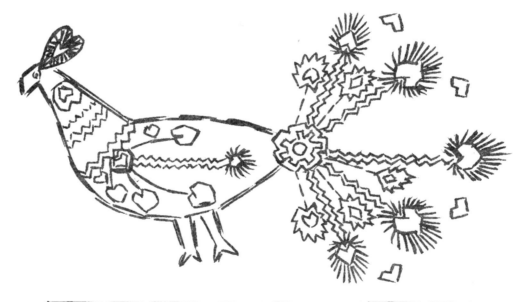

Procedure

1. Fold the 12" x 18" sheet of colored paper lengthwise.

2. Draw one-half of the design on the folded paper, so that when it is cut out and opened up it will form a symmetrical design. (Keep in mind that the edge of the fold will become the center of the design.)

A common leluja design is a pair of birds or roosters near the bottom and an abstract treelike form in the center. Keep the design simple. You can add fanciful flower and leaf shapes and decorative edges to the tree form after the basic shape has been cut out. Also, you may want to shade in the part of the design to be cut away to make sure it is all one piece.

Materials

12" x 18" sheet of colored paper— choose from colored craft paper that comes in large rolls, gum-backed papers, origami papers, or solid-color wrapping papers
pencil
small, pointed scissors
white glue
12" x 18" white construction paper or another contrasting color construction paper, color to match wycinanki cutout (optional)

3. Use small, pointed scissors and cut out the wycinanki. It is sometimes easier to cut in from the edge using curved or wedge-shaped cuts.

4. When the cutting is finished, open up the wycinanki and glue it to a sheet of white construction paper or another contrasting color.

5. The white construction paper can then be glued to an even larger sheet of construction paper in a color to match the wycinanki.

(You may wish to begin by trying this procedure with newsprint or newspaper before using the colored paper circles.)

1. Fold the circle in half with the colored side *inside*. Fold it in half again two more times. This will give a pattern of eight repeats. This folding will create a wedge-shaped piece with folds on both sides.

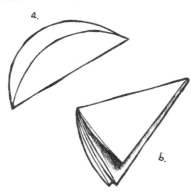

2. You will create your design by cutting into both folded edges as well as the curved outer edge. You may want to cut freehand, or you can draw your design on the paper, if you wish. As you cut into the curved edge, try to keep the basic roundness of the edge.

Materials

newsprint or newspaper (optional)
colored paper, cut into a circle 6" to 7" in diameter for small designs and 12" to 14" for large designs. Choose from thin, colored craft paper that comes in large rolls, gum-backed papers, origami papers, or solid-color wrapping papers
small, pointed scissors
white glue
white construction paper
thin cardboard—shirt or poster-board thickness (optional)
thin acetate (optional)

3. Open and glue the completed gwiazdy wycinanki to a larger square of white construction paper with a margin of at least ¾" on the sides and 1¼" at the top and bottom.

4. If you wish, glue the framed design to a thin piece of cardboard cut to the same size. Then cover the design with a thin sheet of acetate. Cut the acetate larger than the design, wrap it around to the back, and secure with tape.

 # Potatoes with Cheese Jackets

Ingredients

butter or shortening to grease cookie sheet
one-pound can small whole white potatoes
¼ cup grated Parmesan cheese
¼ teaspoon paprika

Utensils

cookie sheet
can opener
measuring cups & spoons
small bowl
mixing spoon

Procedure

1. Preheat oven to 400°F.
2. Grease a cookie sheet.
3. Open the can of potatoes. Drain potatoes and set aside.
4. Combine the cheese and paprika in a small bowl.
5. Roll the potatoes in the cheese mixture.
6. Place the potatoes on the buttered cookie sheet. Bake for 15 minutes.

 # Red Cabbage and Apple Salad

(Makes 4 servings)

Ingredients

2 cups of red cabbage, grated
salt
1 apple, grated
1 small onion, chopped
sugar
pepper
salad oil

Utensils

grater
measuring cups
plate
sharp knife
medium mixing bowl
mixing spoon

Procedure

1. Place the grated cabbage on a plate and sprinkle it with salt. (This will make the cabbage soft.)

2. When the cabbage is soft, mix it with the grated apple and the chopped onion.

3. Sprinkle with a pinch of sugar, a little pepper, and a little salad oil. Mix well and serve.

 **Barszcz**

(Makes 1½ quarts)

Ingredients

(The first 3 ingredients are used to make beet kvas.
   The beet kvas has to set for 2 to 4 days.)
5 to 6 cups boiling water
3 cooked beets, sliced
½ cup vinegar
****
1 cup beet kvas
5 cups meat or vegetable broth
2 tablespoons brown sugar
rye bread (optional)
sour cream (optional)

Utensils

measuring cups and spoons
paring knife
medium saucepan
mixing bowl
strainer or slotted spoon
large saucepan
spoon

Procedure

(Beet Kvas)

1. Pour boiling water over the sliced beets and add vinegar. Let stand at room temperature for 2 to 4 days.

2. Drain off the juice to make 4 cups of beet kvas. Discard beets.

(Barszcz)

3. Heat beet kvas, meat or vegetable broth, and brown sugar to boiling. Skim surface, if necessary.

4. Serve hot or chilled with rye bread and a dollop of sour cream.

Kapusniak
(Makes 10 servings)

Ingredients

2 pounds pork shanks, ham hocks, or pig's feet
1 quart water
1 medium onion, sliced
1 bay leaf
5 peppercorns
sprig parsley or ¼ teaspoon parsley flakes
1 pound sauerkraut
2 cups meat broth, bouillon, or meat stock
8-12 ounces bacon or smoked link sausage, diced
        (optional)
¼ cup raisins or 2 tablespoons sugar (optional)
3 tablespoons flour
3 tablespoons margarine (room temperature)
½ teaspoon salt
¼ teaspoon pepper

Utensils

measuring cups & spoons
5-quart kettle with lid
large spoon
paring knife
slotted spoon
strainer
small mixing bowl

Procedure

1. Cook pork shanks in water in a 5-quart kettle for 20 minutes. Skim off the foam.

2. Add onions, bay leaf, peppercorns, and parsley. Cook for 45 minutes or until the meat is tender.

3. Remove the meat from the broth. Strain the broth and return it to the kettle.

4. Remove the meat from the bones. Discard the skin and bones. Dice the meat.

5. Rinse the sauerkraut with cold water and drain.

6. Combine diced meat, sauerkraut, broth, bacon or sausage, and raisins or sugar. Simmer for one hour.

7. Mix flour and margarine to make a smooth paste. Stir into simmering soup. Cook and stir over medium heat until thickened. Mix in salt and pepper.

8. Serve with plain boiled potatoes or dumplings.

Poppy Seed Cake

(Makes 2 loaves)

Ingredients

Cakes:
3 eggs
2½ cups sugar
1½ cups milk
1 cup plus 2 tablespoons oil
1½ teaspoons almond extract
1½ teaspoons vanilla
1½ teaspoons butter flavoring
1½ teaspoons baking powder
3 cups flour
1½ teaspoons salt
1½ tablespoons poppy seeds
Glaze:
1½ teaspoons almond extract
½ teaspoon vanilla
½ teaspoon butter flavoring
¾ cup sugar
¼ cup orange juice

Utensils

large mixing bowl
mixing spoon
measuring cups and spoons
2 loaf pans (grease and flour pans)
small mixing bowl

Procedure

1. Beat eggs in a large mixing bowl.
2. Add the remaining cake ingredients to the beaten eggs. Mix well.
3. Pour into two greased and floured loaf pans.
4. Bake in a 350°F oven for 50-60 minutes.
5. While cakes are baking, mix all glaze ingredients.
6. Cool cakes for 10 minutes. Carefully remove from pan. (Cakes will be warm.)
7. Pour glaze over warm cakes. Cool before slicing.

 # Noodles with Poppy Seeds

Ingredients

egg noodles
salt
6 tablespoons softened butter or margarine
⅔ cup poppy seeds
1 cup sugar
1 lemon rind, grated

Utensils

large saucepan
colander
measuring spoons and cups
grater
mixing spoon

Procedure

1. Cook noodles in lightly salted water. Drain well.

2. Add butter or margarine and mix well to prevent the noodles from sticking. Keep hot.

3. Mix sugar, poppy seeds, and lemon rind. Sprinkle over noodles.

4. Stir to mix. Serve at once.

 **Pisanki**

Materials

hard-boiled egg (Although raw eggs are generally used, hard-boiled eggs have been substituted because drying raw eggs takes up to one year.)
soft sponge
pot of beeswax
pan of water
hot plate or stove
drawing paper
pencil
crayons or markers
paintbrushes (various sizes)
dipper
food colors in cups or small bowls for dipping
candle
tissues

Procedure

1. Clean the hard-boiled egg with a soft sponge and allow it to dry.

2. Place a pot of beeswax in a pan of water. Heat it on a hot plate or stove burner until the beeswax is melted.

3. Plan a design for the egg on a sheet of paper. Define the shapes and the colors the egg is to be dyed. When you dye, you will want to begin with the lightest color and then continue by using related colors. For example, yellow, yellow orange, orange, orange red, and so on.

4. Use a paintbrush to apply wax to the areas where the white color of the egg shell will show.

5. Dip the egg into the lightest color. Allow it to dry. Then cover any areas of this first color to be protected with wax.

6. Dip the egg into the next color. Repeat the process until all of the colors have been dyed, waxed, and dried.

7. Warm the egg over a candle to remove the extra melted wax. Be careful not to scorch the shell! Polish your egg with tissues.